Preface

Previously, the farmer knew how to use the soil to continue to yield crops. Today, our life is far from many processes that give us food. 2019 was the Year of Greta Thunberg and demands for revolutionary change. Greta Thunberg`s message is revolutionary. Politics are more complicated.

Albert Camus described how people have the choice between apathy or action during a disaster in the "Plague" (1947). The plague was a symbol of the Second World War. Today, the book could just as well serve as a symbol for our refusal to take climate challenges sufficiently seriously. We still have a choice between action and apathy.

I saw Greta Thunberg for the first time on Skavlan, January 19, 2019. I was fascinated by her personality, her words, and her perspective of Asperger`s.

The history of Greta Thunberg is a history of commitment, excellent spin, and how media work today. Greta Thunberg, being a social and political phenomenon, also questions politics versus movements, lobbyism, and campaigns.

The political landscape is more complicated than ten years ago. In 2019 climate activism had a good year and made headlines more often. Much thanks to Greta Thunberg`s campaign. In 2020 and the years to come, the climate has to answer to more than headlines. Greta Thunberg`s campaign gave the climate more than five minutes in the spotlight, but what`s counts are results.

It is a critical book, but it is not a negative book. Climate is important. A sustainable climate is crucial for the world. The importance of international cooperation to solve the climate`s many challenges can hardly be rated high enough. We all depend on each other – as humans and countries. Yet, there have never been more questions about international cooperation. Brexit in the United Kingdom. Donald Trump in the white house, and the rise of populism both in the US and Europe. To find a solution to the climate in this landscape will not be easy.

Greta Thunberg made headlines in 2019. Who is she, and who were important for her place on the world stage? I will hardly get the last word about Greta and the spin of the century. So many smart people have believed the story about the lonely girl with the homemade poster. Her story cries for an alternative analysis of the story.

I am a Norwegian lecturer and author. I have a degree in political science and education in dramatic art. I mean, a sustainable climate is important. It is also important that politicians don`t get fooled by green lobbyism. Climate change is also about big money. Every sane politician ought to take climate change seriously. But not to get fooled!

Arendal /Oslo
Åse Thomassen

Content

A SWEDISH ICON

The word *icon* originally comes from Greece and has had a religious function in the Byzantine church and later as art. Today, we often use an icon as a concept without having any connection to the Church, history, or art. The term icon often refers to people who symbolize something through their personality, position, or work. Persons who almost become a metaphor for something greater than themselves, where the person often symbolizes something more than the person. Mahatma Gandhi. Nelson Mandela. John F. Kennedy.

Internet and globalization offer many opportunities to create products and symbols. Barack Obama became the symbol of change in America and around the world. His simple rhetoric: "Yes, we can" made a great impact. Together with his rhetorical talent, he became the symbol of change in the US. And hope. He even got the Nobel Peace Prize in Norway less than a year after he became president of the United States of America in 2009.

Ingmar Kamprad managed to make Swedish simplicity be an important part of the core values of IKEA, even after it had become a successful company worldwide. Sweden is a complex society. It was indeed a mind of a genius that converted "simplicity" from the little place Älmhult with a concept for furniture from Ikea. Simplicity is also a keyword in Greta Thunberg`s campaign.

Values and appearance are important for leaders. It is important to signal values creating thrust. Throughout time, humans have cultivated icons. Answers may be lacking in people`s lives. Answers may be lacking in politics. On the other hand, the cultivating of people and politicians who appear as icons. An image of the person that is larger than the person.

Until recently, Sweden was the picture of the perfect society. With a good business life, a successful welfare state, Volvo and Ingmar Bergman. Immigration, violence, and bombs have changed something in the image of Sweden. Sweden is nevertheless still a successful society with a welfare state.

Greta Thunberg is Swedish, but very unlike many Swedes, both young and adult swedes. The combination of her looks, braids, and seriousness is something out of the ordinary. Still so ordained. She is a kid, soon to be a young woman. But the pictures of her dwell on the child. Her youth as an image of a pure soul. She is very different from the average teenager, which is not bad at all. It is still something disturbing with a youth dressed like a much younger child. It is very unlike a Scandinavian youth in their mid-teens.

Scandinavian countries are pure in many ways. Truth is more common than in other societies. It is more thrust between the state and the people, and a low degree of corruption. The society where Greta Thunberg grew up. A Scandinavian country where the majority trusts the authorities. There are great similarities with neighboring Norway where I live.

There are many types of staging. We know it from politics, fashion, theater, and movies. From Cleopatra to John F. Kennedy. From princess Grace to princess Diana. President Macron in France managed to make many people believe in him when he ran for the election in 2017.

In a theater, it is easy to understand when the performance begins. The audience expects nothing else. Staging in society and organization is something else. It is about what an organization or a politician wants people to see. A politician wants to show his or her good sides. A typical example of staging is a politician with his wife and children. Traditional family values. Less typical: President Vladimir Putin, who shows his strong body.

After a sex scandal, the next step for a politician is often a press conference with their wife. After a sex scandal, they make a performance about the devoted husband and his forgiving wife. This is staging – nearly elementary staging. Staging can also be harder to see through. Boris Johnsen has become Prime Minister. Before he became Prime Minister, it was not always easy to see when he was a clever politician or just a clown in politics.

Greta Thunberg has become a climate icon after a very short time. The staging of Greta Thunberg may have drawn inspiration from two other Swedish icons. The first is Astrid Lindgren`s Pippi Longstocking. The second is Stieg Larsson`s Lisbeth Salander, a role character who is strongly inspired by Pippi Longstocking. Common to both is that they master life even though their starting point is more than difficult.

Pippi Longstocking is a fictional nine- year- old girl. She has a big house, Villa Villekulla. And a horse and a monkey. Pippi is strong and independent. Pippi Longstocking has red hair and pigtails. She is an unusual supergirl, able to lift a horse with her arms. She is both kind and playful. She often makes fun of adults. Pippi Longstocking is an adventure of a girl, even though she lives alone. Her life is stories about friendship, mood, and mastery. Her red braids became iconic.

The readers seldom discovered that she was a lonely child. Her life seemed so warm, cheerful, and life-affirming. Few understood that Pippi was a lonely child living alone. A Swedish icon. A fantasy of fun and superpower for children all over the world.

Stieg Larsson`s Lisbeth Salander is an atypical hero in a crime novel. Her features and social form have captivated readers and film audiences across the world since 2005. So alone in the world, and yet such a strong and determined young woman. She has friends. Still, she struggles with communication. With Lisbeth Salander, mastering is a keyword. She is a superb hacker with the ability to solve puzzles, either alone, or with the journalist Mikael Blomkvist. The books and films about Lisbeth Salander are fiction where a hopeless start with violence, social and psychological problems, nevertheless provides adventurous opportunities for the leading lady. Lisbeth Salander shows mastery - at a high level of hackers. The author Stieg Larsson named her flat after Pippi Longstocking`s house, Villa Villekulla.

When Greta Thunberg started with her strikes for a better climate on 20th August 2018, she was 15 years old. In Scandinavia, 15 years is an age between child and adult. In her mid-teens, a time that for many is characterized by exploration of existence. Greta Thunberg is different, both in clothing and attitude. It is perfectly ok, but it gives a picture of av childish youth. Her appearance often has similarities to younger children than her age. In many of the photos, she looks like a lost child. That has partly changed with fame during 2019.

Greta Thunberg is a very serious youth. She is concerned with the climate with the same dedication as athletes who train to win the Olympic Games. For other young people, however, it is important to be young, teenagers. After a year on the World Scene, she has a less childish image. She became a young woman in 2019.

In several of the photos of Greta before the summer in 2019, one can see a visual shadow of Pippi Longstocking, as if she was related to this strong Swedish icon. It`s is hardly a coincidence. After the summer of 2019, her image changed. Greta Thunberg performed with her hair in a long braid. For nearly one year, she had many similarities with the image om Pippi Longstocking. The strongest girl from Sweden. Pippi Longstocking has been a great Swedish icon for more than 70 years. The staging of Greta Thunberg with similarities to Pippi Longstocking was hardly a coincidence. It was staging. The supergirl for a sustainable climate. A supergirl with pigtails like Pippi Longstocking. For nearly one year from August 2018 till July 2019.

The pigtails were almost a trademark for Greta Thunberg in her first year of climate strikes. It has changed. But the image of Greta Thunberg alone, outside the Swedish Parliament Riksdagen, with braids, has long since become the public image of Greta Thunberg. It`s a very clever staging of the third Swedish icon for strong Swedish girls. But unlike Pippi Longstocking and Lisbeth Salander, Greta will save the whole world – from climate devastation. She lacks the mood of Pippi Longstocking. Like Lisbeth Salander, she is devoted to her work and doesn`t talk if it is not necessary.

A GREEN (ECONOMIC) REVOLUTION?

Green energy, green politics has become a part of a greater good. Climate and green values are both important. At the same time, it is important not to be fooled by all kinds of green businesses. Climate change is also about business.

The temperature rises. States, politicians, and people alternate between action and apathy. Climate change destroys. We can repair damages after a storm. It is more difficult to make an island habitable again.

Climate is important. The survival of the planet is important. A sustainable climate policy depends on all countries in the world. Climate has been an issue for decades, but the world can still do better. We all depend on each other, as humans and countries. Former Prime Minister in Norway, Gro Harlem Brundtland, was chair of the UN – appointed Brundtland commission. The report was published in London in 1987. The report got lots of attention. But here we are, still lacking solutions for a sustainable climate.

There is still a lot we do not know about the climate. Cause and effect have not been determined once and for all. We still don`t know enough about the sun`s impact on the climate. Much research is undone. In the meantime, we must emphasize the climate in politics locally, nationally, and internationally. The planet needs no less care than our home. The globe is our home.

Not only as a metaphor but also in reality.

The French philosopher Raphaël Enthoven has named Greta an anti-product. He says:

"When you consume Greta, you do not help the planet. You play the game of the system that destroys it".

Enthoven has a point. Greta Thunberg is indeed a product of our time. Even if she is a committed climate activist, she is also a kind of secular saint. Her activism is not about money. I am not sure that is the case with the clever people who helped her to the spotlight. A green shift is also business and big money.

It can be a soft line between climate activism and climate as a business. Greta Thunberg is in the middle of many interests, twice in Davos – the Mecca of Money. Other places as the savior for the climate, presumably with no hidden agenda.

Greta Thunberg stands for rhetoric that sounds alarmed. She is, at the same time, unresponsive to our society. Still, she is treated by many as a top politician, something of a western answer to Dalai Lama. It is not a criticism of her; on the contrary, I blame the adults who leave a teenager to be the index finger of our time. There is reason to ask if the combination of money and activism around Greta Thunberg is a fair game – for society. Who profits from what? Where is the transparency?

Malena Erman, Greta`s mother, hoped for a #metoo campaign for the climate. She wrote about the opportunities such a campaign could have for the climate(Erman, Ernman, Thunberg, and Thunberg,2018) in her book about the family. The dramaturgy of Greta Thunberg`s rapid road to fame has similarities with #metoo. A campaign that probably had its peak in 2017. Since Malena Ernman wrote she wanted a #metoo for the climate, the family had a goal. The dynamic in media and social media also driven by technology and different factors in the media. The two campaigns did not come from anywhere. Feminists had worked for women`s rights. Dedicated people and all kinds of activists had worked for a better climate in five decades. All these people made a difference when #metoo and Greta Thunberg became world-wide campaigns in 2017-2018(#metoo) and 2018-2019(Greta Thunberg and FridaysforFuture).

Of course, a sustainable climate is important. Thomas Chr. Wyller asked already in 1999 whether the necessary turnaround operation is possible within a democratic system or whether a revolution is necessary. If you listen carefully, Greta Thunberg`s speeches are revolutionary. We cannot cheer for her message without debate. Greta Thunberg asks us to listen to science. Science about the climate is important, so is science in general. Greta Thunberg`s rapid journey to the world`s foremost scenes should interest political scientists and marked scientists for years. These are questions for the behavioral sciences. Given that perspective, this book is just an appetizer.

TALKS AND RHETORIC

In this chapter, I will analyze the speeches Greta Thunberg gave in 2019 and her speech in Davos in 2020. I suppose Greta Thunberg wants us all to understand the speeches just as they are delivered. Given her status and many platforms, it is important to analyze her speeches. She wants an impact on society – without any election. Her speeches are her instruments between her and the world stage. What exactly is her message?

The three cornerstones of the rhetoric are logos, ethos, and pathos.

Logos is about the factual argument in science and debate. Logos presupposes that we have the same understanding of concepts. When Greta Thunberg talks about science, it seems that she takes for granted that everybody has the same understanding of science as her. Not all science meets the requirement of truth and objectivity according to the ideal of Aristotle. In society, on the other hand, we often assume that factuality is truthful, although many politicians will say that five apples are seven. Other politicians will say that there are only two apples. The truth is that it is always five apples in this example. She knows too little about the many dilemmas in science. After all, science is about new knowledge that makes previous knowledge less relevant – or not relevant at all. At the same time, much knowledge is the same as it was 100 years ago. Greta Thunberg talks about science as if it were laws instituted by God. All research is not as constant as the formula for the circumference of a circle. Science rejects yesterday`s knowledge and research every day. Science is anything but static. For politicians and leaders, it`s about having the most up-to- date knowledge about climate and other relevant issues. All science is not suitable for application in politics. There is no easy road from science about climate till politics for a sustainable climate.

Logic is important in an argument. When Greta Thunberg speaks, she gives the impression that her speech is logical. Science is not always pure logic, even if objectivity and logic is an ideal in science.

Ethos is about the nature of the speaker. For politicians, for example, it is important to emerge as people with good and respectable qualities. For Greta Thunberg, it`s about being a young person who has recognizable values about the importance of climate. Young people often seem more genuine than adults.

Pathos is about arousing feelings and commitment from the audience. Greta Thunberg`s school strikes are an effective use of pathos. The lonely, sad child. The homemade poster. And a great ability to speak about the necessity of acting for a sustainable climate.

The rhetoric of fear is both known and little known. Since ancient times, we know that fear can give leaders more power. State leaders turn to an external enemy through politics, rhetoric, or war. The context that creates fear caused by various causes can, be unifying in a country. A state leader acting on fear can gain increased support through the rhetoric of fear. President George W. Bush played on the rhetoric of fear after nine eleven. He talked about the axis of evil. Bush used the term for the first time in his State of the Union- Speech January 29, 2002, to describe regimes that supported terror.

There is, of course, a big difference between Greta Thunberg and former President George W. Bush. What they have in common is that they play on fear. Many would probably think that it is an unreasonable comparison, but it is not irrelevant for that reason. Where former President Bush fear rhetoric appeared to be cynical, many would not think the same about Greta Thunberg`s rhetoric. She is flimsy and still a child. It is easy to underestimate a child.

Within the framework of rhetoric, Greta Thunberg`s speeches have a simplified language. She constantly refers to science as if it was the only truth. The history of science is a story of some truth that last for centuries. New research can reject the truth. Greta Thunberg has stated that science is "rock- solid." There she exaggerates. Scientists cannot say rock- solid without reservation. Few truths last forever. The research on climate, of course, indicates that we must take the climate threat seriously. It is not the same as that all research on climate will be valid in the future.

Her speeches are both authoritarian and utopian. Her rhetoric has similarities to dictators and seducers of the public. Her speeches give a picture of an apocalyptic situation where only radical measures will be good enough. In a speech in London in April 2019, she identifies with Extinction Rebellion. It is a very radical and extreme, nonviolent organization, which puts climate ahead of all other political issues. When she arrived in Europe with a boat, in December 2019, the next boat in the harbor had the flag for Extinction Rebellion. Perhaps a coincidence. Perhaps not. Extinction Rebellion uses different methods. Both perspectives on climate change are extreme.

"The real power belongs to the people" is a well- known slogan from the 1960s. Before the sixties, this was new and partly unknown rhetoric, except the speeches of the trade union movement and political parties on the left in the 1960s.

Greta Thunberg asks for a change. Climate gets much more attention. Said by a child, her message sounds normal. She asks for drastic changes, nearly demand for revolutionary changes. The Norwegian writer Kaj Skagen (2019) believes Thunberg appears to be a person with one-track thinking, blind to nuances, and controversy. She assumes that the climate is the only thing that matters, according to Kaj Skagen.

Several of her speeches have the same basic structure. They consist of simple, short sentences. The content is all about:

- That the adults have failed
- The solutions are already known
- Science has all the answers
- We have all the knowledge we need
- Adults are immature
- Children take responsibility by striking
- Children should not take responsibility for the adults

All her speeches are pretty much the same, with a few of the points in every speech. Greta Thunberg is a clever performer And a terrible one as well. Her talks are partly outstanding. Her voice is clear. She is partly an excellent speaker. Yet, she is also a vulnerable and shy teenager. That is part of her charm, but also a problematic issue. Who is Greta Thunberg in this complicated mosaic of a teenager, and a celebrity on the world stage?

Those who have directed Greta Thunberg`s path to success know that she is a child with many challenges. It is not only the many challenges of climate that create her desperation. When she arrived in New York, August 28, 2019, she seemed both happy and relieved, also uneasy. Many contradicting feelings.

Her first speech at the COP 24 in Katowice in 2018 is controversial. She spoke for a nearly empty room, late in the evening.

She starts by introducing herself. She then draws the analogy between a small country like Sweden and children. She says both Sweden and children are examples of the possibilities to make a difference. Although both Sweden and children are small, it is possible to make a difference, says Thunberg. She calls for clarity and action. Already in Katowice, in December 2018, she said that adults are not mature enough, leaving the burden to the children. She also talks about changing the system to bring about the necessary changes.

The audience, if anyone was present during her speech, can hardly have understood the revolutionary message of Thunberg. It is easy to underestimate children. On the other hand, it is interesting how she deprives adult morals. She says children`s moral is superior to adults. That is only a statement from Greta Thunberg.

Greta Thunberg spoke at the World Economic annual Conference in 2019. Approximately 3000 people attend the annual conference. She sat in a chair and read from the script. The audience is top leaders from business and politics. She sits with pigtails and clothes that are strikingly outdated. The performance in Davos was five months after she sat down outside the Swedish parliament.

Two years earlier, on the annual meeting in World Economic Forum, in Davos, they discussed how they should think to a greater extent in the long term, and not regard profits as the main and only goal. There, based on the capitalist thinking prevailing in Davos, it was almost like inviting a revolutionary to the annual meeting. Greta Thunberg`s demand for reducing emissions will require a radical transformation of society and politics. Read her words and see what it says. It is a radical message, which many people underestimate when a skinny girl with pigtail and outdated clothes sits on the stage and talks.

"*Our house is on fire, I am here to say our house is on fire. According to the IPCC we are less than 12 years away from not being able to undo our mistakes.*

In that time unprecedented changes in all aspects of society needs to have taken place including a reduction of our co2 emissions by at least 50% and please note that those numbers do not include the aspect of equity which is absolutely necessary to make the Paris agreement work on a global scale. Nor does it include tipping points or feedback loops like the extreme powerful methane gas being released from the thawing Arctic permafrost.

At places like Davos people like to tell success stories but their financial success has come with an unthinkable price tag. And on climate change we have to acknowledge that we have failed. All political movements in their present form have done so. And the media has failed to create broad public awareness. But Homo sapiens have not yet failed. Yes we are failing but there is still time to turn everything around we can still fix this, we still have everything in our own hands. But unless we recognize the overall failures of our current systems we must probably those probably don't stand a chance.

We are facing a disaster of unspoken sufferings for enormous amounts of people and now is not the time for speaking politely, we're focusing on what we can or cannot say. Now it's the time to speak clearly. Solving the client crisis is the greatest and most complex challenge that Homo sapiens has have ever faced.

The main solution however is so simple that even a small child can understand it. We have to stop the emissions of greenhouse gases. And either we do that or we don't. You say nothing in life is black or white but that is a lie, a very dangerous lie. Either we prevent a 1.5 degree of warming or we don't. Either we avoid setting off that irreversible chain reaction beyond the human control, or we don't. Either we choose to go on as a civilization or we don't. That is as black or white as it gets.

There are no gray areas when it comes to survival. Now we all have a choice. We can create transformational action that will safeguard the future living conditions for humankind, or we can continue with our business as usual and fail. That is up to you and me.

Some say that we should not engage in activism, instead we should leave everything to our politicians and just vote for change instead. But what do we do when there is no political will? What do we do when the politics needn't are nowhere in sight?

Here in Davos, just like everywhere else, everyone is talking about money. It seems that money and growth are our only main concerns. And since the climate crisis is a crisis that has never once been treated as a crisis, people are simply not aware of the full consequences of our everyday life.

People are not aware that there is such a thing as a carbon budget, and just how incredible small that remaining carbon budget is. And that needs to change today. No other current challenge can match the importance of establishing a wide public awareness and understanding of our rapidly disappearing carbon budgets that should and must become a new global currency in the very heart of future and present economics.

We are now at a time in history where everyone with any insight of the climate crisis that threatens our civilization and the entire biosphere must speak out in clear language, no matter how uncomfortable and unprofitable that may be. We must change almost everything in our current societies. The bigger your carbon footprint is, the bigger your moral duty. The bigger your platform the bigger your responsibility.

Adults keep saying we owe it to the young people to give them hope. But I don't want your hope, I don't want you to be hopeful. I want you to panic, I want you to feel the fear I feel every day. And then I want you to act, I want you to act as if you would in a crisis. I want you to act as if the house was on fire, because it is" (Greta Thunberg).

The facts of the speech are few, limited to what may emphasize that we are on a cliff of eternal destruction in a few years. Thunberg does not have perspectives on how we should act, only that people should panic. As rhetoric, that`s dramatic. As a fact, panic is not desirable for anyone. It can act as a very good metaphor, make one think. In reality, panic is neither a feeling nor a situation in which to make the best decisions. The combination of the slim girl in the chair on stage and the dramatic message of the speech created excitement and were quite special.

TED x Stockholm started with her first understanding of climate when she was eight years old. The beginning is very personal.
She wants to put a stop to fossil fuels since it is harmful to the climate. She sees the problem completely detached from the context of fossil fuels in society. She focuses unilaterally on the adverse effects. Her form is the rhetoric of propaganda. Unilateral, without reservation.

She became ill at 11 years old. She uses her depression to explain her commitment to the climate. Since it is a speech, no doctors can tell her that there is no causal link between the climate and her depression. That`s just her explanation. It is an argument disconnected from society`s knowledge of depression.
She claims that autistic people are the "normal ones." It is wishful thinking or a metaphor. As if being autistic gives a clearer mind. That is not logical. As rhetoric, it is a strange way to get the rhetorical upper hand. But it works as rhetoric. Since she is young and vulnerable, she does not have to answer factual questions about the logic of the benefits of autism.

Malizia 2 was a very symbolic journey. Rhetoric is not only what you say but also what you do. It is not a free lunch. For a politician, rhetoric is not only what he or she tells, but also choices made, especially choices that show deviation between life and learning. Greta now has a public position that is subject to the same spotlight politicians and other public figures meets. Therefore, the choice of Malizia 2 to bring her across the Atlantic is interesting. It shows that Greta is happy to work with rich people if it promotes her personal goal of not flying. The crossing was a big PR stunt for Greta Thunberg and the owners of Maliza 2. Both parties received a lot of free advertising. Her journey gave more emission since a new crew had to fly to the United States to sail the boat back to Europe. If the goal was publicity, the trip was a success for the owners and Greta. If her goal was to avoid emissions, the result was the opposite. She caused great emissions with the journey. Far more than a flight for her and her father, Svante Thunberg. In terms of PR – a top result. When it comes to rhetoric, it shows that Greta does not always live as she teaches. Her reluctance to fly gave the world a larger amount of emission. She has not given a logical explanation for this choice.

Greta Thunberg participated in The Daily Show with Trevor Noah on September 14, 2019. The TV program is a mixture of news and entertainment. When she arrived in New York, she felt the smells, and tells it is pollution, she explains in the show. On the boat across the Atlantic, she smelt nothing except sweat. It`s two funny descriptions of smell. Of course, there was more smell on the boat than from sweat. Smells are not just something negative, like sweat and pollution. Smells are also smell, from the sea and people on the boat. In New York, there are other smells than that of garbage and unhealthy products and processes.
It is, of course, unfair to read too much from an interview. Most of us are not precise when talking. A conversation is not always just logical. We don`t mention all that is relevant. Nevertheless,

Greta Thunberg`s description of smell tells us something about her way of understanding the world. She saw the negative by smell(sweat) when she was on the boat and the negative by smells when she arrived in New York. It is not wrong, but it is only a very limited picture of the smells at sea and the many smells in a city like New York.

Thunberg explained that she did not fly because of the emissions. She also said that she did not care that her mother had to change her profession because Greta did not want her to fly as an opera singer.

Greta Thunberg believes that adults and older adults do not care about the climate because they will die anyway. It`s a bit of an exaggeration. It is hyperbole in rhetoric. She also attributes adult motives when she describes their motives as inferior to the younger population. It is descriptions that may fit Greta Thunberg`s action on Fridays, but it is probably not true that adults look as cynically at climate issues as she describes. She said about adults thinking:

"I won`t be alive anyway, so screw it."

Many adults do not have the power to take responsibility for the climate. On the other hand, I do not know anyone who is as cynical as what Greta Thunberg repeatedly repeats. Adults care about the future of children and grandchildren. They could have done more, but it`s incredibly rude by Greta Thunberg to say that adults think they`ll die anyway, so they don`t care about the future.

Greta spoke at the Youth Climate Conference organized by the UN on September 21, 2019. One year and one month after the campaign started outside the Swedish Parliament, she speaks with authority. She refers to everyone who has demonstrated for the climate and then says that young people are united and cannot "be stopped". It is a strong message – also as rhetoric. No one can deny that millions were striking for a better climate all around the world on September 20, 2019.

When she spoke after the strike in Battery Park in New York on September 20, she said that the future had "been stolen." She said like she has said many times before:

"Why should we study for a future that has been taken away from us?"

"That has been stolen for profit!"

She demands that politicians act. In her words, it gives a clear sense of action. She says that politicians cannot act without the demands of the youth. She gives the young people a rhetorical ethos, which the politicians seem to lack if we should take what she says literally.

The speech in UN September 23, 2019, was a combination of theater, a punishing style reminiscent from evangelical preachers from previous centuries. Rhetoric without respect for adults. The speech was structured around:

"How dare you!"

It is a rhetoric that we know from a darker Christianity. Before this rhetoric was typical in alternative Christian movements. It`s a kind of rhetoric where the audience can expect to be punished for all their sins. It`s not a forgiving God in this rhetoric.

The speech was directed but not adapted to a young person`s body language and language. Between the dark rhetoric, the studied facts, one could see a vulnerable child on the edge of an emotional plunge.

Greta Thunberg held a speech at the UN Climate Change Conference in Madrid, COP 25, on December 11, 2019. The speech is both impressive and characterized by the formulations of others, partly adult perspectives. It is also her universe, of course. It has a few facts and criticism of politicians and leaders. The perspective is the adults who have experienced the world. She ends the speech with: "We the people." Indeed, a new kind of totalitarian populism.

Greta Thunberg visited the World Economic Forum for the second time in January 2020. She gave her best speech in Davos. It was clear, pinpointing facts and her battle for the climate. Still extreme as in 2019, but a bit more down to earth regarding the relationship between goals and means. She blames "all" for not achieving the goal of the Paris Agreement.

Greta Thunberg has a strong message in Davos. She continues to blame everyone. She talks about the children and the people as if they are more fit to master the climate challenge.

The rhetoric that I still doubt is her own is fascinating. Like:

" From a sustainability perspective, the right, the left, as well as the center, have all failed. No political ideology or economic structure has been able to tackle the climate and environmental emergency and create a cohesive and sustainable world. Because that world, in case you haven`t notices, is currently on fire."

Her words, her age, her body create confusion. What she tells the word leaders are that they are all useless. At school, that would have been bad behavior. In Davos, it is a golden speak. Strange and paradoxical. That does not mean that Climate challenges don`t demand our attention.

As in 2019, "the house is on fire". She concludes in 2020:

"Our house is still on fire. Your inaction is fueling the flames by the hour. We are telling you to act as if you loved your children above all else"

Indeed, a strong message. Clever use of metaphors. At the same time, it is up to grey politicians to find solutions, as well as businesses to develop and use more climate- friendly technology.

The icon of revolutions, Che, is still the icon of liberation and revolution of the last century. History has shown that Che was not a hero. When I listen to the speeches of Greta Thunberg, it strikes me how brutal they are, and how revolutionary the content is. The many who pay tribute to her today cannot listen very well to her speeches. Or is it actually true that young people want a social revolution in the name of climate?

Her speeches all revolve around the same themes. The sentences are short, and the message is tough and almost brutal. The adults are to blame. The good morale only by young people. It`s elegant as rhetoric. Not as sincere and true as Greta claims to be. The speeches are her reality, not the world as it is for politicians, businesses, and all the ordinary people around the world.

Greta Thunberg draws a simple moral map. And although many could have done more for the climate, she is drawing a far too black picture of adults. She means business with her speeches. In Battery Park in NY, she said that they didn`t strike for politicians to take selfies together with them. She demands politicians to act. She says nothing about how.

THE TEAM

Greta Thunberg and her parents protected the idea of the lonely girl outside the Parliament as if they had a patent on reality. The management behind Greta Thunberg has triggered both rumors and facts. Greta Thunberg has not worked alone. It started in Stockholm in the spring of 2018. Greta Thunberg came in second in an essay competition for school students. Bo Thorén from Fossilfritt Dalsland (Fossil Free Dalsland) invited her and other young participants to a brainstorming about actions for the climate. For a long time, it had been a desire for young role models in the climate fight. The young participants were presented with several proposals for actions. School strikes were one of the suggestions presented. The idea of a school strike was an idea from the US. Students protested against gun laws after the school shooting at Parkland High School.

Greta Thunberg was the only one of the youths who thought that school strikes for a better climate were a good idea. From that perspective, the image of the unknown girl with a homemade poster is not entirely real. Not quite true. It`s not the same as saying that Greta`s fight is not real. It is more about the story are more complex, with several actors involved in everything from the idea to the implementation of the campaign.

Ingmar Rentzhog is a Swedish entrepreneur and successful businessman. He started a new company, to support the Climate as a reaction to Donald Trump being elected US president in 2016. He founded and is CEO of We Don`t Have Time. It`s a tech company aiming to become the largest social media platform in the world for the climate crisis. Nothing less.

Ingmar Rentzhog, who took part in Al Gore`s education program Climate Reality in Denver, is one of 12 000 leaders in 135 countries. He was by no means a random passer-by when he met Greta Thunberg outside the Swedish parliament Riksdagen when she started the school strikes.

Rentzhog was a key player in Greta Thunberg`s first phase of the school strike for climate. When Greta Thunberg sat outside the Swedish Parliament, August 20, 2018, Rentzhog brought a photographer. The photographer took the iconic pictures of" the lonely girl with the homemade poster." Ingmar Rentzhog later admitted that he was informed one week before Greta Thunberg started her strike for a better climate. In an email exchange with Andreas Henriksson, Rentzhog said that he used his company We Don`t Have Time to help Greta Thunberg with:

- Spread the news about Greta globally
- Spread the news in the world`s news media
- Help her with Facebook
- Help her with Twitter
- Produce videos on Youtube

This information contrasts with the story about the lonely girl with pigtails like Pippi Longstocking. Indeed, this was professional PR from day one.

Amazingly, already in Davos in January 2019, there were questions whether she was working alone. Even in Davos, she had supporters that wanted people to stop asking questions about the persons behind her. It did not seem like any red lights flashed when the allegations came in Davos in January 2019. Normally "davosites" are defined by their belief in economic and social liberalism, and their positions on the top of organizations, many of them are leaders of global organizations. It was probably only "natural" that a 15-year-old girl gave a speech for the world`s leaders at the World Economic Forum in Davos, one might think. Of course, it`s not common. Although the campaign around

Greta Thunberg made headlines in the media before the end of 2018, it is a bit from there to an invitation to speak in Davos in January 2019. There are busy people with tight schedules attending WEF in Davos. It requires careful planning. There is little time for spontaneous invitations, one might assume. While speaking in Davos, Greta still collaborated with We Don`t Have Time, which is led by Ingmar Rentzhog, and who is the magician in the story of Greta Thunberg. Indeed, he had time, for her campaign! The lonely, skinny girl against the world.

Svante Thunberg is a former actor. He was a manager of his wife Malena Ernman before Greta`s campaign took off. Now he is Greta`s manager. It was a little weird to see him backstage in the boat when Greta arrived in New York. As an actor who looks at the audience before the show begins. At the same time, he does not have a defined role in the public. He is the background while Greta Thunberg, his daughter, is the star. Like his wife was before.

Kevin Anderson is important in Greta Thunberg`s work. She has several professionals and volunteers who help her and give her input. The foremost contributor is undoubtedly the British climatologist Kevin Anderson. In an interview with Spiegel Online, Anderson says that Greta submits texts for comments, and ask him to check the professional content for any errors. He says he perceive her as a younger colleague. Professor Kevin Anderson also shows his support for Greta Thunberg on Twitter.

Malena Ernman, Greta`s mother, has an unclear role. She is not visible in contrast to Greta`s father. Since Greta became known, her mother has made her two daughters co-authors of the book. Greta is also actively used on the cover of the book and in marketing.

Malena Ernman has been promoting the book since August 24, 2018. It was published four days after Greta sat down in the front of the parliament building. The book weaves the family crisis with the climate crisis. In connection with the book Malene Ernman said:

"We burn out on a burned out planet"

It is a phrase that bears great resemblance to Greta`s rhetoric in her speeches.

Today, pop stars sell effects and clothes. The Thunberg family sells a book that hands out information about their daughters. It seems to work. The book is translated into several languages. The book does not have a high level as a book, or a good language sells like hot wheat bread. Fame is often a trigger for sale.

Recently it was revealed that Malena Ernman wanted the Swedish national broadcasting (SVT) to produce a program about Greta Thunberg and her family, already in 2016 (Expressen, October 7, 2019)

Beyond the book, the mother`s role is unclear, although she is still the mother of Greta Thunberg. She had also changed career since Greta did not want her to fly, something her career previously demanded when she was an opera singer on several of the world`s stages.

Daniel Donner, who works as a lobbyist in Brussels, is Greta Thunberg`s press spokesman. He works in The European Climate Foundation.

Fridays For Future is an interesting organization. The website #FridaysForFuture has no name for contacts in Sweden on the website. As if no one runs it or is responsible for the website. It`s only information from countries participating in the strikes and two email addresses for the media. In a way, it seems like a website that drives itself. Of course, that`s not true.

Contact information is limited to this email addresses:

international.media@fridaysforfuture.org

swe.media@fridaysforfuture.org

The website tells:

"#FridaysforFuture is a peoples movement following the call from @GretaThunberg to school strike".

#FridaysForFuture is a professional web site. Therefore, it is rather striking that there is no contact information with names. Apparently, someone is running it. Still, the organization of the site is almost a mystery. There are many claims that Greta is leading the school strikes. She hardly does. Thunberg inspires the school strikes. Hardly as a leader. It may seem that way now, but many have also done a solid job, one can only guess the range of it. There is hardly any reason to believe that Greta Thunberg has been the actual leader of FridaysforFuture. Her role is limited to her speeches. Her role is probably more symbolic than practical.

Per- Anders Stoknes is an example of role mixing. In his position associate professor at BI Business School in Oslo in Norway, he talks about Greta Thunberg as an academic. He is also on the board of directors of We Don`t Have Time. When he promotes Greta Thunberg in his position as an academic on BI, he omits to mention his role in the company We Don't Have Time, the company that was so important in Greta Thunberg`s first phase of her campaign. Per- Anders Stoknes is also an active member of the green political party, Miljøpartiet de Grønne. He is a deputy representative to the Norwegian Parliament. He has met 218 days in the Parliament, Stortinget, since 2017. His PR for Greta Thunberg is indirect. His objectivity is problematic. So is his impartiality. When he is an expert in a TV studio, he is under the label, associate professor at the business school BI.

Greta Thunberg`s journey started through cooperation with green business interests and brilliant PR. It was secrets about her and the help she received. There is every reason to expect that everything is not known today. Greta, both honest as a person, but also staged, already in the first photos August 20, 2018. The narrative presented by Ingmar Rentzhog. As with pop stars, there is often a manager behind the band. Greta Thunberg has had and still has several advisors and associates, from her parents to professionals like Ingmar Rentzhog and Professor Kevin Anderson. The lonely girl with a homemade poster is beautiful. Reality is far more complex.

PARENTS AND ETHICS

Most of us are not perfect parents. As parents, it`s easy to understand that it is unfair to criticize other parents. Being a parent is not about being perfect. It`s about doing the best for the children. Make them feel safe and loved. Greta Thunberg`s parents Malena Ernman and Svante Thunberg, seem to be an unusual combination. Loving parents. No need to doubt their love for their daughters. But at the same time, without boundaries about their daughter`s place, identity, and history in society. They seem to fail as parents, both when it comes to exposing their daughters, and also by giving out their daughter`s diagnosis in the book about the family. Greta told the world: How dare you! (UN September 23, 2019). In a distant future, she might have reason to ask the same question to her parents.

The different illnesses of Greta and her younger sister have received wide publicity after their parent`s book was published on August 24, 2018. It is important to be open about illness, but openness about your own children's illness is quite far more than what`s rational and ethical. The children have a whole life ahead of them. When they meet new people, people will know their diagnoses. That`s not the best start in a relationship; other people are knowing something they don`t need to know. Normal parents would not do something like that. It`s about ethics, the hidden contract between parents and children.

The first of September 2019 Greta Thunberg posted this on Twitter:

"Before I started school striking I had no energy, no friends and I didn`t speak to anyone. I just sat alone at home, with an eating disorder. All of that is gone now, since I have found a meaning, in a world that sometimes seems shallow and meaningless to so many people".

This quote shows that the path from a life of hopelessness to stardom can be very short. It also tells us how problematic Greta Thunberg`s public role is. It is not always clear where her suffering begins and ends, and if her fight for climate is just a fight for a better climate, or a part of her pain as a person. Her mental challenges are woven into the climate struggle. Not unlike the situation of some of the greatest artists in history. Pain does not only have misery as a result. Greta Thunberg is just in the early stages of her life. What happens after an intense year in 2019, nobody knows.

The Danish historian and journalist Mikael Jalving wrote: "The family is in deep crisis and the mother has not understood at all. The book should not have been published, according to Jalving. The family should instead have received help. The book is a cry for help "(Berlingske Tidende, May 27, 2019). Jalving says he wanted to report the mother to the police when he read the book. Like me, Mikael Jalving, cannot understand that a teenager can benefit from having her history of suffering posted to public view. Jalving believes that children ought not to be presented as a Climate Jesus. He believes it is the adults who are responsible and that children who save the world are a performance from the fairy tales. Mikael Jalving also looks at the book as a caricature. I purposely call Malena Ernman`s book "The book." As I see it, the book is not a legitimate project as a book. One can probably ask: What is wrong with parents hanging out their children for a whole world? As parents, that is something they never can undo. Imagine when their daughters get romantically involved, and their boyfriend will know everything that`s "wrong" with Greta or her sister from the very start. It`s pretty cruel.

"The book" draws almost equal sign between the climate and the family`s trouble with different challenges. Psychologist Ole Jacob Madsen says in the newspaper Aftenposten that it is wishful thinking. Of course, that is what it is: wishful thinking. Or an excuse for not coping with a very difficult reality in the family.

Malena Ernman and Svante Thunberg may probably have the best intentions with everything they do, from the book to Greta`s role in the climate battle. It would be absurd if I were to condemn them for their choices. It should also be allowed to ask questions of parents who make such radical choices on behalf of their children. So far, Greta Thunberg`s climate activism has been a success story. No one knows when the spotlights get turned off. Greta has challenges. Today, Greta says it`s a gift to have Asperger`s. It is not a gift, even for Greta Thunberg. She even said she sat alone and friendless before she began the climate strike. Her diagnosis does not go away with success. The diagnosis will give her challenges for the rest of her life.

Her father, Svante Thunberg, is her manager. It`s far from ordinary life when the youth is the star, and her father is backstage. It is a circus in the media where Svante Thunberg is both circus director and trainer of his child. It is, for sure, a debatable role for a father. At the same time, Greta Thunberg has become a clever public speaker. Svante Thunberg`s role is more characterized by being in the shadow, but always close to the spotlight that surrounds his daughter.

Since she is not an adult, her parents have to travel with her. Her father`s role will continue to fuel all kinds of speculations. Greta insists that she write her speeches, but the speeches have the rhetoric and words of an older person with skills in rhetoric. All the time, Svante Thunberg stays in the shadows of her daughter, silent as if he is a soldier in the Mafia. What her father does as Greta`s manager can only be told by him. Now, it almost like relying on "indices" to understand the actual role of Svante Thunberg.

MEDIA AND SOCIAL MEDIA

When something goes viral in our time, a lot can happen quickly. The Norwegian party SV(Socialist/populist) nominated Greta Thunberg for the Nobel Peace Prize less than six months after Thunberg sat down outside the Swedish parliament for the first time August 20, 2018. The Norwegian political party argued that climate is the biggest threat in our time. They regarded, therefore, Thunberg`s work worth the prestigious Nobel Peace Prize. How could social media and media transform an unknown 15 years old into a star in a few months? What is the recipe?

"Funky Business" showed already twenty years ago that the world works differently in a global market. If you have a product that reaches the market, there are new and different possibilities. Global trade has changed into something quite different from before. Within the framework of "Funky Business," it`s possible to understand new products and new phenomena. To understand how Greta Thunberg became famous in a short time, one has to understand how global markets work. It is also crucial to understand how media and social media work.

In the book by Greta Thunberg`s family (2019:189), they write about the inspiration from #metoo. It`s interesting. There are several similarities between #metoo and Greta`s rapidly rising fame. A lot of the dramaturgy is similar. The combination of spin, a clear message, media, and social media can be an explosive cocktail. Greta Thunberg`s journey from loneliness in her room to recognition around the world took only a few months. These are both campaigns marked by a huge drive and little room for disagreement with the message. #metoo was important for women, but also led to false allegations. It is not unreasonable to assume that Greta`s campaign also could have negative side effects. Like children fear the climate threat in a way that is not good for the child`s health. Both climate and feminism have many active people in different organizations. That matters when a campaign like Greta Thunberg`s starts rolling.

A few people knew for some time about her plans for striking outside Riksdagen, the Swedish Parliament. Ingmar Rentzhog was informed a week before. He visited her and posted an update on Facebook. The two newspapers Dagens Nyheter and Aftonbladet, wrote about Rentzhog`s mention of Greta Thunberg the same evening. The beginning of a viral success started less than a day after Greta started her strike.

Ingmar Rentzhog wrote this August 20, 2018:

"I want to share an emotional morning with you. The day begins with delivering my three-year-old son to his new department in kindergarten. He is sad. He will not be left alone in the new department in kindergarten. After a hard goodbye where he does all he can to try to show me that he is not sorry and that he fits in, I go to work with a bad feeling in my stomach.

On the way to work, the road goes past the Parliament. There, Greta, 15 years old, sits striking alone against the whole world."

"We children don`t often do what you say we should do, we do as you do, and like you adults, shit in my future, so do I. My name is Greta, and I am in the ninth. And I am a school striker for the climate until Election Day."

"This is what Greta Thunberg says," continues Ingmar Rentzhog. "and that the adult world must act is the big questions today about our destiny."

"Her school strike starts today and continues until Election Day. She sits in front of the parliament building. During the time I was there, only one passerby came forward and took her flyer. No one except I talked to her.

Imagine how lonely she must feel in this picture. People were just walking by. And continuing with the business as usual. But the truth is. We can`t, and she knows it!" (Ingmar Rentzhog, originally written in Swedish) A sad emoj followed his post about Greta Thunberg.

Indeed, rhetoric with the ability to move. Ingmar Rentzhog shows that he can write a text that both can move and inform. It seems so casual and yet so good as PR for Greta Thunberg. He shows that he is a good man(ethos), with thoughtfulness for his little son and Greta. His son in the nursery. Greta outside the Parliament building, Riksdagen. Indeed, a man of our time.

Ingmar Rentzhog also joined the strike on August 24, 2018. He posted photos of his participation in the school strike on the pages of his company on Facebook and Instagram. I don`t know if anyone reacted since Rentzhog is a little bit too old to strike from school. Of course not, he only did his job as CEO for We Don`t Have Time.

Twitter is a very effective "broadcaster." A tweet can have a great impact in less than a second. When Ingmar Rentzhog`s company We Don`t Have Time, wrote the first tweet about Greta Thunberg August 20, 2018. The following persons and companies were included in the tweet:

*Greta Thunberg

*Zero Hour (youth movement)

*Jamie Margolin (teenage founder of Zero Hour)

*The Climate Reality Project (founded by Al Gore)

* People`s Climate Strike

The tweet said:

"One 15 years old girl in front of the Swedish parliament is striking from School until Election Day in 3 weeks.

Imagine how lonely she must feel in this picture. People were just walking by. Continuing with the business as usual. But the truth is. We can`t, and she knows it!"

A photo of Greta Thunberg outside the Swedish parliament followed the text in the tweet. A very clever staging of the lonely girl with a strong message. It is not untrue, but a skillful manipulation of reality. She was not as alone as the photo. Ingmar Rentzhog shows that with simple linguistic means, he can play on emotions, the ethos, and pathos of rhetoric. He created the image of the brave little girl against the world.

August 20, 2018, Greta Thunberg wrote on Instagram:

> "We children most often do not do what you ask us to do. We do as you do. And since you adult`s shit in my future, so do I. I strike from the school for the climate until Election Day (translated from Swedish)."

August 20, 2018, she was unknown to the public except for being the daughter of her parents, the singer Malena Ernman and her mother`s manager, Svante Thunberg. Magically, everything in Greta`s life changed one day in 2018, if we believe the script.

Greta Thunberg has 9,7 million followers on Instagram in January 2020. Before her journey to the US in September 2019, she has 3,1 million followers on Instagram.

An article on the Norwegian website "Naturpress" was published the first day Greta Thunberg sat down outside the Swedish Parliament. Usually, only big news become known in Norway on the same day as in Stockholm. Before Dagens Nyheter (the biggest Swedish Newspaper) published the article about Greta Thunberg on August 20, 2018, in the evening, this was not news in Stockholm or the neighboring country`s capital, Oslo. An article on a Norwegian website is an indication of networking before Greta Thunberg started her strike. The moving image of the lonely girl described by Ingmar Rentzhog was thus, in many ways, an illusion. A processed picture of the actual situation. A great spin.

Ingmar Renzhog participates in many finance and climate activism networks. He was the "founder" of the product Greta Thunberg with the first photo from August 20, 2018.

The company We Don`t Have Time has developed an app that makes it easier to communicate around the world. Climate crisis and communication are two important keywords for We Don`t Have Time, which was founded and led by Ingmar Rentzhog.

Social media can be considered a jungle where most people do not reach a particularly large audience. The clever spin behind Greta Thunberg found the media`s autostrada to celebrity status in less than four months. Of course, Greta herself had significance. But without skilled backers who knew the media game, Greta`s strike could have ended after three weeks, as she originally planned.

A UNIQUE TEENAGER

Greta Thunberg is no doubt a fabulous girl, and a young woman. In an age when children insist that they are grown, and in the next moment are relaxed as just being children. In Norway, Sweden`s neighboring country, you are an adult from 18 years- old. There are great similarities between Norwegian and Swedish culture, including the youth culture. Most 16-year-olds are between pre-adult and child. Greta Thunberg stands out from the crowd of young people.

Greta is no doubt both clever and dedicated. She has lots of charm. She has shown the whole world many of her emotions, from crying to positive feelings like smiling, relief, and proudness. And sometimes her sense of humor.

She has had many struggles in her young life. Living without a correct diagnosis could not have been easy for the even younger Greta. She has gone through difficult years. She talks about her past problems as if it is every day for both her and the world. Depression and eating problems are not normal in society. Still, it is nice that Greta almost mentions it as usual. Ordinary. That`s important for everybody suffering from depressions and eating disorders.

The young girl we see now is often a clever performer with a better English than many people from the countries in Scandinavia. She is a clever young woman.

What separates success from failure are, in many cases, will. And the will to implement. Greta Thunberg has shown an extraordinary willingness to do what she thinks is important. Although there is much to criticize when it comes to the people around Greta Thunberg, one cannot take from her a unique commitment. She deserves our respect. Her commitment seems honest. Her determination is genuine. The many who talk about what they want to do, without acting, can learn from Greta`s determination.

In most social issues, many have opinions, but many do not translate opinions into action. That`s what Greta Thunberg does. In all societies, you will find people who would rather talk than act. No one can take from Greta Thunberg her passion for the climate. Her willingness to do something, with climate as she regards as very important. There she stands apart from all the talkers in the world, of course with important exceptions.

Greta Thunberg has a simple and unadulterated charm. It`s easy to like her. In the bright light of medias spotlights, one can also see the very young woman who both likes to act, but at the same time, she is not comfortable with all the attention. She does what she thinks is right, even when it is unpleasant for her as a person.

In this chapter, my ambition is to say whats positive about Greta Thunberg, but there at still many reservations. Her parents have taken a great chance by letting her have this form of self- realization at an early age. But maybe there might be no reason for worries. Perhaps her success as a climate fighter is just the beginning of an adventurous life.

This book questions the spin around Greta Thunberg. It`s not as if I question her. She is a fabulous girl, soon to be a young woman. Her determination is her superpower.

MANIPULATION OF FEAR

Greta Thunberg`s rhetoric emphasizes the demand that we panic. It works well, rhetorically. Rarely anyone is asking us to panic. It is more often a condition that comes due to conditions that individuals and communities do not have control over.

All times have conditions that can create fear. Generations have heard the stories of wars and the danger of nuclear weapons after the Second World War. Many feared the nuclear bomb, but no one encouraged anyone to panic. On the other hand, informational films produced to calm the population. As, for example, that it would help with a blanket against the effects of the atomic bomb. There are indeed no blankets in the menu Greta Thunberg serves. She wants people to feel the fear with their whole body, as she does. It is not a positive proposition. It makes no sense to feel fear. It is, of course, possible that Greta uses it as a rhetorical tool in her speeches. She is saying that people should sense true fear like hers in their bodies. It is not a sensible proposition. Her fears are her fears, not something she should encourage others to feel.

Over the years, there was a growing recognition of the need for sustainable development and protection of nature. It did not lead to strong feelings, and political parties often allowed growth to win over various environmental needs when making decisions. Norway, being a good example of this kind of politics. Scientists and politicians have known the need for sustainable development for more than 40 years. Where Greta Thunberg`s rhetoric is extreme, politicians in the past may have had too little rhetorical appeal to the human side by climate. Politicians are also afraid of not being re-elected if they emphasize climate more than their voters do.

One can choose to see the positive in the cultivation of Greta Thunberg. She undeniably brings the climate issue higher on the agenda. But it also has a scary aspect. It is rather negative rhetoric, not characterized by mastery. Where a Pippi Longstocking could show us our way to a solution in a cheerful way, Greta Thunberg has little else to offer on a society's lack of mastery. She gives no hope. Just wants us to panic. The fact is, most societies are not ready for a rapid change. It is about politics, technology, and resources to choose sustainable solutions. Greta Thunberg does not accept that fact – as a fact.

The movie "The Wave" from 1981, directed by Alex Grasshoff, is interesting in this context. It is a dramatization of a contentious social experiment at an American high school in California in 1967. "The Wave" showed the suggestive power of propaganda, but also the frightening result of propaganda. The students were ripped off by the propaganda. In the end, they were disappointed when they realized it was a bluff, staged by their teacher.

Greta Thunberg wants people to panic. When she talks about panicking, it seems like she expects panic to result in rational choices. People who work with people who experience panic (their house is burning) or panic as a part of a mental condition, can tell that panic and rationality often can be found on two different roads, two very different roads.

Panic is not the best button for rational behavior. It can, for sure, lead to the opposite of rational behavior. Panic is:

Sudden uncontrollable fear or anxiety, often causing wildly unthinking behavior.

Greta Thunberg may not be thinking about the crippling panic. Or the confusing panic. Her rhetoric seems to understand the panic that something that will change behavior as if humans were robots that respond to danger with rationality. One knows little about human nature if one believes that panic about the Climate will generate reason. People are not that simple. Emotions are not that simple. Society is not that simple. Politics is not that simple. The latter is, of course, a challenge for important and necessary decisions on climate and sustainability to be made. Not only regarding Greta Thunbergs`s revolutionary speeches and demands for change.

Ella Whelan (2019) writes: "But the admiration for this rather eccentric young woman`s protest also sends a rather worrying message about the current state of adult authority; It is strange that teachers, politicians, and parents are cheering on children whose message is: "I`m too scared to go to school."

One should not read Greta Thunberg as the devil reads the Bible. Nevertheless, it is relevant to say that Greta`s apocalyptic message can scare, confuse, and give children and young people less hope for the future. Today, many are concerned about children striking. They count the number of striking children and young people. No one, or very few, asks how the kids are coping. In what way they can make a difference. Which choices they can take, both as humans and consumers.

GRETA THUNBERG AND POLITICS

Greta Thunberg gives no doubt attention to the work for a better climate. At the same time, her speeches and demands for action could have possible side effects. She rebukes and blames, but it is the politicians who must solve the climate challenges, of course, in addition to the businesses or cooperation with the business world.

The climate challenges require leadership and prudence from politicians. So far, Greta`s extreme message has led to polarizing rather than good solutions to our real climate challenges. Politicians meet her like she was their equal. They give her platforms and respect, but when the performance is over, the results of every day count more.

Her campaign has many possible side effects. These are some of the challenges that may come.

1. Young people may lose hope
2. Reactions like in the film "The Wave" (previous chapter)
3. Young people stop believing in society
4. Young people get problems with anxiety
5. Politicians act without adequate planning to show that they have climate ethics
6. The demand for quick solutions can lead to unnecessary

    polarization
7. Symbolic climate solutions
8. Choosing solutions that do not have a proven effect on the climate.
9. The focus on Greta Thunberg can make people tired of the debate on climate

Work for a better climate is important for many reasons. Research tells us that we must take the consequences of our negligence due to several risks. Politics must be debated, criticized, and decided. It is nothing for Greta Thunberg to decide. She is a symbol, not an elected politician. It is politicians in different countries and international organizations that must decide policy for the planet. The left side of politics is often shocked by the rise of populism. Greta Thunberg has many similarities to populism. Her message is also authoritarian. What she has in common with populists is a simple ideology. Her one-dimensional demands are hardly realistic in terms of both climate and politics. Well, climate should have a more important position in the politics of states. But there is nothing that can happen based on a marching order, without nuances and options for action.

Thunberg`s message is so extreme that it can seem divisive and frightening more than leading to necessary work and cooperation for political solutions. The phenomenon Greta Thunberg has already led to a huge polarization between those who want to give her authority, and those who see the weakness or the staging of Greta as a young front figure. Many people are angry – but of different reasons. Some people don`t accept work for the climate. That is only stupid, but even they are voters. They have a voice.

Politics is a struggle between different political parties. It is basically that all political parties want the best for society, even if their ideology, rhetoric, and political tools are different. Greta Thunberg has just one goal- a sustainable climate. It`s difficult not to understand what Greta Thunberg wants. She wants action to save the climate. It is politicians who must make decisions. It requires both will and time. In politics, it`s rarely about snap one`s fingers, as if reality was a waiter.

The difference between ordinary politics arises when it comes to the complexity of politics. Political science has countless examples of how difficult it is to achieve goals as they originally were intended from the political decision-makers. Greta Thunberg acts as if there is no complexity in politics. She asks for action. Ordinary politicians, on the other hand, must consider the economy and different challenges. And they must not act in a way that can prevent them from getting reelected.

Today Greta says that adults "are not mature" and that the youth must take responsibility for them. It`s easy when it`s all about taking time off from school and protesting in the streets. That day young people will do something significant for the climate; it will be about politics because young people in the streets can be nothing more than a press group. It is likely many young people will become disappointed. Politics is more complicated than demanding action. In 2019, Greta and the youths received a lot of attention to demand action. Practical politics are rarely glamorous. Young people may have an unrealistic perception of politics and decision making. Only dictators can demand action NOW! Politics in democracies take time. Both voters and politicians must be convinced of the choice of solutions that emphasize a sustainable society and climate. It`s easy for Greta to call for action. In practical politics, convincing voters and political parties take time. A Sustainable climate is important. Politics is complex. Politics need more time than Greta Thunberg`s revolutionary time schedule.

DAVID AND GOLIATH

The battle between David and Goliath is classic. In Norway, most people will agree with David, the little one against the giant. Lee Child says he is passionate about the story of David and Goliath. Unlike Norwegians, he is fascinated by Goliath. His figure Jack Reacher is the thrillers' response to Goliath. He is grappling with all obstacles of the world, which are obstacles to his quest for a solution to the mystery.

Greta is, in many ways, the story of David. Or the little girl who dares to challenge the giant. However, that picture is incomplete. Those who have pulled the threads have a closer kinship to Goliath than David. Both big money and green shareholders are not as visible as "the little girl who stands up to the power". In a way, the story of Greta is both the story of David (Greta) and Goliath (Ingmar Rentzhog and his network). Yet it is only the young woman – Greta- who makes tough demands on the politicians. Many shareholders are not on stage.

Greta Thunberg is an interesting case that will require further research from several disciplines to form a fairly true picture of what has happened on the stage and what has happened in a small selection of directors of the great PR around Greta.

When it comes to Greta Thunberg and her crew, plus those working behind the curtain, it is more unclear who is David and who is Goliath. There are strong economic interests in the green shift. Who works with who is partly visible and most of all invisible. When the Swedish journalist Rebecca Weidmo Uvell pointed out mistakes, Greta Thunberg's parents alternated between denying and changing facts. Much of what happens around Greta Thunberg is not transparent processes. Her father is outside the spotlight around Greta. He is also her manager like he was for her mother for 15 years. His role as her manager is still unclear. The child being the star of the family is extraordinary. Malena Ernman was the star of the family and her father, Svante Thunberg, her manager. The family says as little as possible about his new role in the professional field.

The first year has no doubt been a success story. Greta Thunberg`s fame has become like a pop star. The people who facilitated her success could hardly dream of a better result. A Spin should not get attention if the aim is a success. Much of the spin around Greta Thunberg is invisible.

Global media and social media make the reach for possible success tremendous. Conversely, it is easy to disappear in the jungle by anyone who wants a place in the sun. Anyone who wants a slice of the cake, whether it is about money or attention, has to have an excellent strategy.

Greta Thunberg`s message is neat and simple rhetoric. What is herself and what is staging is difficult to know? She insists on being a child. While others aged 16-17 years insist on being older than their actual age, Greta is the opposite. She repeats and repeats, "We the children".

Greta is by nature smaller than many 16-17 years old. It makes her image as a child believable. Seventeen years old is, of course, still a child, although many at that age are impatient to become adults.

Greta has no doubt become an icon. It wasn`t, of course, obvious that it would develop that way. If Ingmar Rentzhog from the company We Don`t Have Time had not included a photographer August 20, 2018, the image of Greta might never have been embraced into an icon.

Ingmar Rentzhog is an important key to explaining the rapid

spread of Greta Thunberg`s message. He is a successful business-man in Sweden. He is also a member of Al Gore`s Climate Reality Organization. His use of social media in the first phase was like launching a rocket to investigate a specific place in space. It was a masterpiece of networking through multiple channels. Still simple, but few masters the tools like Ingmar Rentzhog. He started working with green industries and climate activism in 2017. He is CEO and founder of the company We Don`t Have Time. His company We Don`t Have Time helped Greta with communication. In 2018 he became chairman of the think tank Global Utmaning (in English: Global Challenge). The company We don`t Have Time aim is communication in a world with a Climate crisis.

Zeynep Tufecki says that logarithms on social media contribute to alignment. When Greta Thunberg`s message got a broad audience, the public started to look like State TV in North Korea. Greta Thunberg could be rude and tell adults to be immature. At some point, the audience was growing without critical questions about Greta Thunberg`s agenda and the people working for her.

"We are still counting!" Greta said to the audience in Battery Park in New York on September 20, 2019. Who "we" are is still not completely transparent. Greta`s journey started with Bo Thorén`s (Fossilfritt Dalsland) workshop for young people in spring 2018. Then Greta`s strike August 20, 2018, where Rentzhog was a key player with his magic PR. Who has held other different roles is still not sufficiently known, except for the persons who are working near Greta Thunberg. This case can be of great interest for tomorrow`s researchers. It`s impossible to get all the answers in 2020.

HOW TEAM THUNBERG FACES THE CRITICISM

"Query their motives, and you risk being accused of "climate denial" or bullying a vulnerable child with Asperger`s." (Domenic Green)

I want to think that most countries have expressions like the Norwegian: If you want to join the game, you must endure the roast. The Norwegian expression is banal, but also sets a standard, which can sometimes seem fair, at other times not. When it comes to Greta Thunberg, she wants it in her way, whether it's about her person, message, or her rhetoric. All criticism seems like hatred for her. As if the criticism is the same as evil intentions.

My interest in Greta started with sympathy for her and the climate issue. It must be legitimate to ask questions about a social phenomenon that is far more complicated than what the audience is allowed.

Greta wrote an answer to the many accusations on her page on Facebook on February 13, 2019.

"As the rumors, lies and constant leaving out of well established facts continue, please share this newly updated clarification about me and my school strike.
Please help me communicate this to the grown ups who lie about me and family so that I can focus on school instead:

Recently I've seen many rumors circulating about me and enormous amounts of hate. This is no surprise to me. I know that since most people are not aware of the full meaning of the climate crisis (which is understandable since it has never been treated as a crisis) a school strike for the climate would seem very strange to people in general.
So let me make some things clear about my school strike.

In may 2018 I was one of the winners in a writing competition about the environment held by Svenska Dagbladet, a Swedish newspaper. I got my article published and some people contacted me, among others was Bo Thorén from Fossil Free Dalsland. He had some kind of group with people, especially youth, who wanted to do something about the climate crisis.
I had a few phone meetings with other activists. The purpose was to come up with ideas of new projects that would bring attention to the climate crisis. Bo had a few ideas of things we could do. Everything from marches to a loose idea of some kind of a school strike (that school children would do something on the schoolyards or in the class-rooms). That idea was inspired by the Parkland Students, who had re-fused to go to school after the school shootings.
I liked the idea of a school strike. So I developed that idea and tried to get the other young people to join me, but no one was really interested. They thought that a Swedish version of the Zero Hour march was going to have a bigger impact. So I went on planning the school strike all by myself and after that I didn't participate in any more meetings.

When I told my parents about my plans they weren't very fond of it. They did not support the idea of school striking and they said that if I were to do this I would have to do it completely by myself and with no support from them.
On the 20 of august I sat down outside the Swedish Parliament. I handed out fliers with a long list of facts about the climate crisis and explanations on why I was striking. The first thing I did was to post on Twitter and Instagram what I was doing and it soon went viral. Then

journalists and newspapers started to come. A Swedish entrepreneur and business man active in the climate movement, Ingmar Rentzhog, was among the first to arrive. He spoke with me and took pictures that he posted on Facebook. That was the first time I had ever met or spoken with him. I had not communicated or encountered with him ever before.

Many people love to spread rumors saying that I have people "behind me" or that I'm being "paid" or "used" to do what I'm doing. But there is no one "behind" me except for myself. My parents were as far from climate activists as possible before I made them aware of the situation. I am not part of any organization. I sometimes support and cooperate with several NGOs that work with the climate and environment. But I am absolutely independent and I only represent myself. And I do what I do completely for free, I have not received any money or any promise of future payments in any form at all. And nor has anyone linked to me or my family done so.
And of course it will stay this way. I have not met one single climate activist who is fighting for the climate for money. That idea is completely absurd.
Furthermore I only travel with permission from my school and my parents pay for tickets and accommodations.

My family has written a book together about our family and how me and my sister Beata have influenced my parents way of thinking and seeing the world, especially when it comes to the climate. And about our diagnoses.
That book was due to be released in May. But since there was a major disagreement with the book company, we ended up changing to a new publisher and so the book was released in august instead.
Before the book was released my parents made it clear that their possible profits from the book "Scener ur hjärtat" will be going to 8 different charities working with environment, children with diagnoses and animal rights.

And yes, I write my own speeches. But since I know that what I say is going to reach many, many people I often ask for input. I also have a few scientists that I frequently ask for help on how to express certain complicated matters. I want everything to be absolutely correct so that I don't spread incorrect facts, or things that can be misunderstood.

Some people mock me for my diagnosis. But Asperger is not a disease, it's a gift. People also say that since I have Asperger I couldn't possibly have put myself in this position. But that's exactly why I did this. Because if I would have been "normal" and social I would have organized myself in an organisation, or started an organisation by myself. But since I am not that good at socializing I did this instead. I was so frustrated that nothing was being done about the climate crisis and I felt like I had to do something, anything. And sometimes NOT doing things - like just sitting down outside the parliament - speaks much louder than doing things. Just like a whisper sometimes is louder than shouting.

Also there is one complaint that I "sound and write like an adult". And to that I can only say; don't you think that a 16-year old can speak for herself? There's also some people who say that I oversimplify things. For example when I say that "the climate crisis is a black and white issue", "we need to stop the emissions of greenhouse gases" and "I want you to panic". But that I only say because it's true. Yes, the climate crisis is the most complex issue that we have ever faced and it's going to take everything from our part to "stop it". But the solution is black and white; we need to stop the emissions of greenhouse gases.
Because either we limit the warming to 1,5 degrees C over pre industrial levels, or we don't. Either we reach a tipping point where we start a chain reaction with events way beyond human control, or we don't. Either we go on as a civilization, or we don't. There are no gray areas when it comes to survival.
And when I say that I want you to panic I mean that we need to treat the crisis as a crisis. When your house is on fire you don't sit down and

talk about how nice you can rebuild it once you put out the fire. If your house is on fire you run outside and make sure that everyone is out while you call the fire department. That requires some level of panic.

There is one other argument that I can't do anything about. And that is the fact that I'm "just a child and we shouldn't be listening to children." But that is easily fixed - just start to listen to the rock solid science instead. Because if everyone listened to the scientists and the facts that I constantly refer to - then no one would have to listen to me or any of the other hundreds of thousands of school children on strike for the climate across the world. Then we could all go back to school.
I am just a messenger, and yet I get all this hate. I am not saying anything new, I am just saying what scientists have repeatedly said for decades. And I agree with you, I'm too young to do this. We children shouldn't have to do this. But since almost no one is doing anything, and our very future is at risk, we feel like we have to continue". (Greta Thunberg)

Greta Thunberg often uses the ethos of hatred. Greta Thunberg seems to describe all the criticism as "hate." She does not distinguish between people who ask relevant questions and the many vulgarities of the commentaries on the internet. It is not fair of Greta Thunberg to call all relevant issues and criticism for hate. Questions and debates are, of course, part of the open democracies. Although Greta Thunberg believes her case is 100 % legitimate, she cannot refuse people to ask questions, comment, and debate. All debate is not "hatred." Initially, I was very positive about her activism. After a short time, I saw that it was something that didn`t match the image of Greta Thunberg. It`s as if it is not legitimate not to follow Greta`s view on the debate. She says:

" Listen to the science,"

but "science" seems limited to climate research. Her rejection of debate is also a rejection of research about her, the social network around her, and FridaysforFuture.

Social sciences are also science. Still, she`s just a teenager. We might probably not expect her to see her place in an open democracy. Understanding research and democracy takes time and maturity, even for people who have grown up in democracies. If it is not allowed to ask questions and do research on Greta`s campaign, we will break the rules of an open society.

Greta writes:

"Also there is one complaint that I "sound and write like an adult." And to that I can only say; don't you think that a 16-year old can speak for herself?"

She comments many questions by pretending that she does not understand the questions. In a way, she questions the legitimacy of the questions about her speeches. When she answers the question by:

"Don`t you think that a 16-year old can speak for herself?"

She demonstrates that she does not accept the terms of the questions. It`s a gap between the way she speaks and the ways she talks in her speeches. The rhetoric is different. There is no need to be a Hercule Poirot of rhetoric to see that.

The way Greta Thunberg meets criticism has a lot of similarities with debates about immigration and #metoo. It`s so easy to call other people`s points of view for hate. There is no hate in asking questions. The open debate, on the other hand, is the foremost quality of Western democracies. In rhetoric, ethos is important. Greta Thunberg stamps many as bad people, often indirectly. It is not a balanced and fair debate technique. She is a teenager and too young and dogmatic to see climate in a political context. Se should learn more about debate and politics in societies. Although Greta is young, she cannot demand to say everything she wants without questions and debate. She places strict demands on society and political leaders. Then it is only reasonable to have a debate about the goals and implementation of a greener politic. It is difficult to argue since Greta Thunberg is a young person. She talks as if she understands both research, politics, and demand the world to follow her demand for action. She cannot dismiss questions, criticism, and debate as hate. It`s too authoritarian, as is her message to world leaders. Anyone can rarely say so much negative about politics and politicians without getting criticism back. She still has the advantage of youth.

ASPERGER`S

Diagnoses have been different over time. What is taboo has varied. There has been an increasing openness about illnesses and various health problems. Still, there are many taboos around deviations from normal. In societies where many people are looking for the perfect look, the perfect life, there is often a lack of understanding of anything that can hinder "the perfect life."

Transparency has a price when it comes to taboo diagnoses. There are still many prejudices against illness. Especially illnesses that are not limited to the physical in human beings. A successful person and artist like Stephen Fry can tell about his illness. It is more difficult for someone who has a regular job. There are still a lot of taboos around all kinds of challenges, from stuttering to schizophrenia.

I did not want to write anything about Greta Thunberg's diagnoses. She is who she is. A diagnosis should not define a person, whether it is about physical or mental challenges. Diagnosis is something you have, not something you are. Although the idea of openness has the best intentions, there is no control over whether openness leads to the desired result of openness or not. Unfortunately, illness often defines a person. I have seen many unwise, stupid, evil, and bad comments about Greta`s challenges with Asperger`s on the internet. It`s probably about commentators` ignorance, thoughtlessness, and malice. Moreover, openness does not only lead to an enlightened conversation. On the internet, openness about Asperger`s can easily become a meat bone for anyone who wants to be negative.

The Thunberg family has chosen to be open about Greta Thunberg's diagnoses. That one may think is good. Still, it becomes a way to take the defining power both from Greta and society. How would one see Greta Thunberg with or without the diagnoses? Today and the years to come? If the choice was mine, the family should not have been so open. Now the choices are made. The consequences of that are both good and bad for Greta. People take her vulnerability seriously. Others lack empathy for Greta`s various challenges on a personal level.

Greta Thunberg has been open about her Asperger's. In a way, it's great. At the same time, she believes that the diagnosis makes her look clearer than others, and thus can make a significant difference from the unimportant. The problem arises when the critics and defenders of Greta Thunberg fail to see the difference between Greta Thunberg and her Asperger's.

Diagnoses will, to varying degrees, cause people challenges. Greta Thunberg has had several years of problems during her childhood. It has undoubtedly been difficult. Today, however, the openness surrounding Greta Thunberg's Asperger's becomes a form of taboo – for the public. Whether you say something about Greta Thunberg and Asperger`s or not, many will project this knowledge into the debate about Greta Thunberg. Unfortunately, many are unable to distinguish one from the other. The person Greta Thunberg is not the actual diagnosis. She is a talented youth with specific challenges that give her more challenges than normal youth.

Asperger s is a neuropsychological development disorder. It has the following characteristics:

Problems with social interaction with others

Deviation in social interaction with others

Behavioral patterns that are limited or stereotyped

Asperger`s is high functioning autism. There are many highly gifted people with Asperger`s. Many who have had difficult lives as a result of Asperger`s. You will find people with Asperger`s among the most successful. On the other side, many persons with problems. It is also important to underline that it is not Asperger`s alone who makes a good or difficult life. Asperger`s in interaction with other characteristics of a person, family, school, and work. Like all characteristics of all people. Although a trait may seem to define a person, humans are more complex than a trait, a diagnosis, or other traits that characterize the person.

Greta Thunberg uses Asperger`s in her speeches. If it was up to me, Greta Thunberg should be considered Greta. Not a kid with Asperger`s. Her parents chose it differently. The book, which is describing Greta`s diagnosis, was published in 2018. Greta has no choice but to transparency. Her parents made that choice for her and her future.

Greta often says Asperger`s as an advantage. That Asperger`s a gift. That is a rewrite of reality. Although there are several talented people with Asperger`s and various forms of autism, these challenges are not an advantage in themselves.

Greta has repeatedly stated that Asperger`s is a superpower. It is not correct. On the other hand, she may have a point. Several people with Asperger`s can immerse themselves in a field in a concentrated way. Greta has shown that ability, but it`s wrong to call it a superpower.

Greta Thunberg talks about Asperger`s as a noble brand, and the ability to see the world in black and white as an advantage. It is also a rewrite of reality. If you analyze what Greta Thunberg is saying, you will probably see how one-dimensional her thinking is. Not only because she is young, but she let the black and white with her perspectives dominate her speeches and messages. Like other young people, she does not see the complexity of climate and climate policy.

Although we know a lot about Asperger`s today, more research is needed to increase our understanding of this form of high functioning autism. Greta defines Asperger`s as a gift. It shows that she is a proud young woman. Her description of Asperger`s is still not correct. Asperger`s gives people challenges, both when they are children and in adult life. The challenges vary from person to person. The challenges require a lot from both the person who has it and the surroundings.

Although Greta is not right in the fact that Asperger`s is a gift or superpower, it is a bit wonderful that she says so. Too many people focus on the negative with Asperger`s. Greta does the opposite, and although she exaggerates, it`s great that she speaks in the way she does about Asperger`s. She shows that Asperger`s doesn`t have to ruin anyone`s life.

EXCELLENT SPIN VERSUS A GREATER GOOD

"Is it not good that young people strike and mobilize for a better climate?" people would ask. Of course, it is much positive to say about young people's involvement in strikes for a better climate. On the other hand, should we conceal the truth about the background for the strikes?

Today, one can say that the campaign, initiated by Bo Thorén and Ingmar Rentzhog, is very successful. Greta has become a star of our time. Youth march for climate in the streets in many countries around the world. It seems like a mood and interest for a sustainable climate. A mood for Greta Thunberg. She is admired for her simple and pointed speeches. Her grim message creates excitement. President Donald Trump was silent, even when Greta has insulted him. After her talk at the UN conference in September 2019 he made a joke about her on Twitter:

"She seems like a very happy young girl looking forward to a bright and wonderful future. So nice to see!" (Twitter September 24, 2019). She got his attention. Many thought he should give her recognition. That may indicate that something is not right. Does the world's most powerful man have a duty to give recognition to a young girl from Sweden? There is something wrong with the perspectives when it becomes wrong for President Donald Trump not to give recognition to a youth. He had no obligation to do that.

A sustainable climate is, of course, important. It is something many can agree about. Then many will believe that the goal is sacred, though the means of reaching the goal are questionable. Still, it must be allowed to think about how a campaign is staged. The method has consisted of:

1. PR
2. Social Media
3. Greta Thunberg
4. Media
5. Important people who have blessed Greta (The pope, celebrities, former president Barack Obama and politicians)

One may ask if we would be sufficiently critical if the campaign had unethical goals, such as discrimination and persecution of people? I think many people overestimate their ability to be critical. The campaign that has contributed to Greta`s success has led people to believe so strongly in her, that they are closing in on the information that could ruin her image as a young hero. The followers of Greta have many similarities to group thinking. Groupthink is a phenomenon when a group of people get together and start to think collectively with one mind. Social media offers completely new opportunities for group thinking, without the participants necessarily being physically present.

Earlier generations have wondered how Adolf Hitler was able to seduce the masses. Hitler`s propaganda was about propaganda and the staging of external enemies like the Jews. The story could have been different if there were social media in the 1930s. It could have resulted in the end of Adolf Hitler`s power, or more people could have joined Nazism. Of course, this is just a hypothesis. But not hypotheses without a purpose. In Hitler`s time, it was about mobilizing the masses. It is also the case today, whether the goals of the campaigns are ethically worthy or the opposite. But with Internet and social media campaigns can have a very strong impact.

Many people will not hear contradictions about the social network that launched Greta Thunberg`s campaign. Greta Thunberg`s campaign is also not suitable for critical questions. Greta is a bright young woman, but she lacks education and the ability to see contradictions and ambiguity. She talks about science as if science always is 100% true and as if science always is 100% objective. Of course, it is not, even though Greta knows a lot of important knowledge and science about the climate.

Today, it may seem like Greta, and the strikes are an organic movement. In a way, it is. But an important part of the story is professional PR people, where Ingmar Rentzhog perhaps is the smartest player. Climate activists in many countries have participated in the organization of strikes. Greta`s strike has undoubtedly inspired, but others have organized something that in a short time, has the dimension of a mass movement.

METHOD AND METHOD CRITICISM

It is not research. It`s a book. Still, I have the researcher`s perspective when I work, whether it is with pure science, articles, or books for the general market. Of course, it is important to limit myself to writing what I actually know about Greta Thunberg and her campaign. My knowledge is limited to:

1. Greta Thunberg`s talks
2. Articles
3. News
4. Interviews with Greta Thunberg
5. Science

I have checked the information in several places, and used source criticism, especially where the sources do not have a proven reputation over the years.

It is easy to make mistakes in all the information about Greta Thunberg. Fake news about her. Incorrect rendering of events is something else that requires careful research. It is, therefore, necessary to check information in several places.

Studying Greta Thunberg is like studying a ship on a way to a destination that has not been decided yet. Greta`s original goal was a school strike for three weeks before the Swedish parliamentary elections in 2018. Her goals have been changing along the way. What was a Swedish school strike, has now become an international movement for young people.

The observant reader will see that I have not written much about FridaysforFuture. It`s because the information of the movement is unclear. It is assumed that Greta has a leadership role. It`s hardly not more than her talks. The responsibility for the co-ordination of FridaysforFuture is still unclear. A future research project could probably study the organization of Fridaysfor-Future. Today, there is too little information about the actual organization. The media keeps saying that Greta is leading Fri-daysforFuture. It is most likely wrong. That she is a figurehead and inspirer is something else. Her role is thus more like the speaker and preacher than an actual leader. For future research, this should be interesting to study.

When studying an organization, it is smart to know the goals of the organization. Greta Thunberg`s goals have been changed sev-eral times since August 20, 2018. The fact that FridaysforFuture now appears as a grassroots organization may be true, but it is not certain. To be able to provide knowledge about this, research is required. And good research questions.

Metoo had its roots in feminism and gender equality. Greta Thun-berg became a player in a field where different movements had been working with the environment for decades.

Although #metoo and Greta`s campaign revolve around a widely different phenomenon, there are major similarities. It should be interesting to study the importance of social media versus the content of the campaign. It should be interesting to study the im-portance of social media for the drive that arises.

AWARDS AND OTHER RECOGNITION

Greta Thunberg has received prices and other acknowledgments since she started her battle for the climate, August 20, 2018.

Prices in 2019

March 8, Woman of the year, Expressen, Stockholm, Sweden

March 22, Rachel Carsons prize, Stavanger Norway

April 4, Golden Camera, Germany

April 12, Fritt Ord 2019 (together with Nature and Youth), Oslo, Norway

May, The Makwan Prize, Italy

June 7, Amnesty International`s Ambassador for Conscience Award

September, The Alternative Nobel Prize, Germany

October 11, This year`s youth hero for the environment, WWF, Sweden

October 29, Nordic Council`s environmental award, *refused to accept*

November 20, International Peace prize for children, Kids Rights Foundation, Netherland. Divina from Cameroon shared the prize

December 4, Right Livelihood Award. The Right Livelihood, Sweden. She was awarded together with other activists

Nomination for the Nobel Peace Prize

March 14, nominated for the Nobel Peace Prize by a left-wing party, SV, in the Norwegian Parliament.

Honorary doctorate

May 23, Honorary doctorate from the University of Mons in Belgium.

Woman of the year in Sweden

March 8, Greta was named Woman of the Year on Women`s Day 2019 in Sweden.

Time Magazine

December, Person of the year, Time Magazine

Greta Thunberg gets awards and recognition quite often now. This overview can, therefore, be outdated rather quickly.

SUMMARY AND REFLECTION

Greta Thunberg is 17. A teenager, soon to be a young woman. Clever. She has a message. A strong message. It is clear, without the adult`s perspectives and reservations. It is difficult to formulate the optimal climate policy, but it is not impossible. Greta`s pointers are important, but she lacks the necessary insight into politics. It becomes more alarm than a starting point for politics. Her understanding of the world is dogmatic and one-dimensional. She blindly thrust science, like a fundamentalist that believes in the bible without modifications and nuances. She is young and lacks the necessary knowledge and insight into the many dilemmas and reservations in research. If we were to follow her logic, the answers were already clear and operational with regards to necessary action. There are no simple solutions to a society that puts greater power on sustainability than it does today. It`s about money, ideas, technology, and political will.

Greta Thunberg is an interesting case, both as a climate activist and a social phenomenon. It is also interesting how god planning, spin, and social media made her famous in less than half a year. It is probably the best spin we will see in a long time. The skill in the spin around Thunberg shows what a powerful tool it is. Although Greta is extreme in many ways, she has no doubt the best of interest for our planet. It is frightening that the same methods can be used by people who lack good intentions. Propaganda was a powerful tool before the internet. In combination with the internet, propaganda is both a fantastic and dangerous tool. Therefore, the reason for

Greta`s rapid fame is important to study, analyze, and understand. It is about nothing less than the struggle between good and evil forces in society, and the tools to succeed with the good versus the opposite. Although I am critical of parts of Greta Thunberg`s campaign, I recognize climate as an important issue, both nationally and globally. Greta is a young activist with an exceptional ability to speak. However, it is not the same as her perspective being correct.

The first of September 2019, Greta posted this on Twitter:

"Before I started school striking I had no energy, no friends and I didn`t speak to anyone. I just sat alone at home, with an eating disorder. All of that is gone now, since I have found a meaning, in a world that sometimes seems shallow and meaningless to so many people."

This quote shows that the path from a life of hopelessness to stardom can be very short. It is, of course, good for Greta. On the other hand, the world`s attention has previously turned out to be a medicine with many side effects. The fate of many pop stars tells many sad stories. It can still be a bright future for Greta. Her strongest currency is her determination. Her strong willpower can also become her enemy if development does not go her way in the short term.

The UN speech on September 23, 2019, showed a vulnerability the world has rarely seen. They – Greta and her family- say "you shouldn`t worry about Greta." Well, that`s all the reason to care. In the UN, her vulnerability came to the surface. She seemed both angry and on the edge of great trouble.

Greta Thunberg is a fascinating young woman, but she is not the solution to the world. She is to single- minded and dogmatic. She is important for the climate issue, even if it was a great spin that made her known in the beginning. At the same time, her rhetoric can create unrealistic expectations, as well as create anxiety and fear in children. How could that happen? How can adults cheer for rhetoric that can scare children and young people? It should be worth more than one study.

This book has not provided sufficient answers on what is Greta Thunberg`s merit and what are the work of NGOs and social platforms like We Don`t Have Time. This is a case that will require research and books for us to fully understand actions before and after Greta began the school-strike August 20, 2018.

References

Caldwell, Christopher (2019): "The Problem With Greta Thunberg`s Climate Activism", New York Times, US

Camus, Albert (1947): "La Peste", Gallimard, France

Clark, Ross (2019): "The trouble with Greta Thunberg", The Spectator

Enthoven, Raphaël(2019): Tweets on Twitter about Greta Thunberg

Erman, Beata, Erman, Malena, Thunberg, Greta and Thunberg, Svante (2019): "Huset brenner", Cappelen Damm, Oslo, Norway

Gorbatenko, Daniil (2019): "The Real Problem with Greta Thunberg is Not Her Age", Foundation for Economic Education, USA

Grasshoff, Alex (1981): "The wave", US

Green, Domenic (2019): " Greta`s very corporate children`s crusade", Standpoint

Lindgren, Astrid (1945): "Pippi Longstocking, Oxford University Press, UK

Larsson, Stieg (2005): "The girl with the dragon tatoo", Norstedts förlag, Sweden

Leith, Sam (2018): "Lee Child: How to write – and get revenge", The Spectator

Nordström, Kjell A. and Ridderstråle, J. (2006), «Funky business,» Universitsforlaget, Oslo, Norway

Næss, Henning (2019): "Den personlige klimakrisen», Ny Tid, Norway

Petring, Louise (2019): "Slagter Greta Thunberg- bog: Jeg har lyst til at melde moren til politiet", Berlingske Tidende, Denmark

Sotirakopoulos, Nikos(2020): "Why Davos loves Greta", Spiked-online.com

Skagen, Kaj (2019:"Ein ny utopi", Dag og Tid, Norway

Stanley, Tim (2019): «Greta Thunberg is selling the rich and eco-lifestyle the rest of us will never be able to afford". The Telegraph, UK

Storrusten, Kristin (2019):" Kan man bli psykisk syk av klimakrisen?», Aftenposten, Oslo, Norway

Sörbring, Karin (2019): «SVT nobbade tv-serie om Greta Thunberg", Expressen, Stockholm, Sweden

Thomassen, Åse (2019):"Få Greta ned fra pidestallen", NRK Ytring

Thomassen, Åse (2017): «Politikk Retorikk Populisme," Protence, Oslo, Norway

Uvell, Rebecca Weidmo (2019): "Ideelt Thunberg," Sweden

Verdibørsen NRK (29.5.2019) Interview with striking school students outside Stortinget, the Norwegian parliament (in Norwegian)

Wheland, Ella (2019): "Why Greta Thunberg doesn`t deserve a Nobel", Spiked

Wyller, Thomas Chr. (1999): "Demokratiet og miljøkrisen", Universitetsforlaget, Oslo Norway

Websites:

Infinitummovement.no

Fridays For Future www.fridaysforfuture.org

Naturpress www.naturpress.no

We Don`t Have Time www.wedonthavetime.org

Afterword

The picture of Greta Thunberg as a child with pigtails was the dominant picture of Greta as a new hero with resemblances to Pippi Longstocking in the beginning. After my article on the website of the Norwegian National Broadcasting Service (NRK)on June 18, 2019, we have seen a change in Greta`s hairstyle. Today she often performs with a braid, not with a pigtail, which was her trademark from the beginning, when her public image had similarities with Pippi Longstocking.

It is 1, 5 years since Greta sat down outside the Swedish Parliament- Riksdagen- august 20,2018. It has been a year of triumph after triumph for her and the campaign FridaysForFuture. Maybe it will benefit the climate. Greta Thunberg has put climate higher on the agenda. In that case, it`s good. We can probably make important and wise choices about climate, but it requires international cooperation. All states must be involved. It will be very difficult, but nothing is impossible. As the doctor, Rieux, in "The plague" by Albert Camus says, the hopelessness of the fight is not a sufficient justification to give up.

Time will show how much damage or good Greta´s negative and alarmist rhetoric has done. It is not Greta`s responsibility, but the people who co- created the Swedish icon for the climate. No matter is so important that it legitimizes to play with young people`s minds. What will happen to all those who have been enthusiastic about Greta`s rather dark rhetoric? We do not have all the answers today. It is often hard enough to be young. Lots of questions to ask about the world and life. Greta Thunberg`s dark rhetoric is not the answer to them, even when she is celebrated all around the world as the very truth about the future for a sustainable climate.

It is possible to have respect for Greta Thunberg as an activist, and at the same time, be interested in the whole picture, which made another Swedish girl a famous Swedish icon. The third after Pippi Longstocking and Lisbeth Salander.

Greta asks us not to have hope. I do not want to follow her wish. There is hope. The solutions will follow knowledge, politics, technology, and resources. Greta Thunberg has given the climate attention. It is, of course, important both for politics and a sustainable climate. At the same time, this was a masterpiece of clever PR. The staging of Greta Thunberg also raises some fundamental questions. Not least about the relationship between activism and lobbyism. And the influence of campaigns in politics in democracies. Not to mention the need for transparency when campaigns want to influence politics fundamentally.

And most of all: What a great spin! By the spin doctors on stage and behind the stage curtains. Greta Thunberg, as a product, is perhaps the best spin of the last decade. It became a social phenomenon beyond Greta Thunberg as a person. No one knows how long Greta Thunberg will remain a star for the climate. Spotlights have a limited duration. No one knows when this story ends.

Although this is a critical book, I want to underline the importance of sustainable climate policy. The planet needs both action and hope. And a discussion about how we live our lives – as consumers. The rest is politics. Innovation and business. And determination to act for a sustainable climate.

www.ingramcontent.com/pod-product-compliance
Lightning Source LLC
Chambersburg PA
CBHW031154250726

48655CB00002B/965

9798614935092